"I purchased your book as a gift for my son who is divorced with a 3 year old son of his own. It has actually helped us both. Great ideas!"

C.T., Phoenix, AZ

"My sister passed away leaving a son and daughter who now live with relatives in California. I am a single guy and had no idea how I would continue to communicate with my niece and nephew. This book gave me some good ideas for keeping in touch. Thanks."

M.E., Chandler, AZ

"Dannette, I received your book, <u>Shorten the Distance</u>, yesterday and read the whole thing today. I have never read a book where so many good ideas and insights could be found in so few pages...well...Joel Osteen might give you a race! You have a wisdom way beyond your years and a heart of gold. Your book displays an uncanny ability to look outside of oneself and to give love to others, with a great tolerance for human frailties and great compassion to forgive and move on. If people would read your book and use even part of your wonderful ideas, I really believe that it could change the world. You have been blessed with many talents and gifts and God has shown you how to share them with others. I am really blown away at your words. Even people in non-separated families could benefit from your advice on how children should be raised. I am really...really glad that I got the opportunity to read your book. Sincerely and gratefully,"

S.M., Houston, TX

"I am an over-the-road trucker; my kids live with my ex-wife in Texas. I was given a copy of this book. Now I have better phone conversations more often with both of them and I have ideas about what to do with my daughter when I see her."

S.S., Shawnee, KS

"I remember you being one of the few kids in a single parent home when we were kids. I'm sure I'd benefit from your insights! Proud of you!"

E.H., Indianapolis, IN

"I like the format. It makes the book very easy to read."

K.R.E., New River, AZ

"I read your book today, got up to page 83. IT'S REALLY GOOD!"

M.K.A., Phoenix, AZ

SHORTEN THE DISTANCE
Nurture your child from anywhere, anytime

Dannette Ellenwood Hunnel

Second Edition

Copyright © 2010 by Lake Rider Publishing
SHORTEN THE DISTANCE
Second Edition
by Dannette Ellenwood Hunnel

First Edition
Best Books USA 2006 Award Winner
Parenting/Divorce
USABookNews.com

All rights reserved. No part of this book may be reproduced, stored in a retrieval system, or transmitted by any means without the written permission of the author.

First Printing by AuthorHouse
Second and Third Printings by
Lake Rider Publishing
Phoenix, Arizona
ISBN-13: 978-0-615-37007-1
ISBN-10: 0-615-37007-1
Library of Congress Control Number: 2010928434

Printed in the United States of America

To Erica, Cheryl and Madison

You have humbled me yet make me proud. You complete me and through you all I have become a better person.

I love you girls!

~

To Gary

For always supporting me when I need to be me,

I love you!

With Great Gratitude

Second Edition © 2010

Expertly, diligently and enthusiastically edited by

Marge Awarski

CONTENTS

Visitation (poem)...11

Introduction...13

The Basics

Parenting..17

Predictability...19

Medical Care..21

Their Home..23

Transportation...27

Siblings...35

The Stepparent...41

Communication and Visitation

Toddlers..51

Preschooler Communication....................................57

Preschooler Activities..63

Kindergarten through 2nd Grade Activities.............69

Daily Reminders..75

Preteens Ages 9-13 Activities and Interests.......77

Summer Visits..83

Extra Curricular Activities.................................87

Social Activities...89

Teens Ages 14-17...91

When Your Teen Comes to Your Home............97

Money...101

Know the Facts..107

Driving...113

Senior Year..115

Birthdays and Holidays

Birthdays Ages 1-2-3.......................................121

Birthdays Ages 4-17..125

Halloween..129

Easter Ages 4-17..135

Thanksgiving...139

Christmas-type Holidays Ages 1-2-3.................................143

Christmas in their Hometown..147

Other Cool Bonding Ideas..153

Epilogue..159

About the Author...161

VISITATION

There is a little part of me

Out in the world so wide,

Who brings to me much laughter, joyfulness and pride.

Does she know I think of her?

Does she know I care?

Does she know how much I wish that I were always there?

I call her every other day to hear her sparkling voice,

There is so much for me to know and much for me to share.

I listen to her stories; I feel those eyes so true.

I say, "I am counting seconds until I'll be with you."

Dannette Ellenwood Hunnel

Introduction

They say write what you know.

After a lifetime of visitation, I decided to make lemonade out of lemons.

Why?

I came from a broken home; my father lived in another city and traveled much.

I had a couple of stepparents.

Later in life I, too, became divorced, and then my children had a father in another state and they also had stepparents.

I remarried and became a joint custodial stepparent to my stepson, his mother residing in another state.

In writing this book it is my intention to help others, especially the children.

Hopefully this book will shorten the distance, bringing parents and children closer together.

THE BASICS

Parenting

"A genitor who does not parent the child is not its parent."

Ashley Montagu

Parenting is a forever thing.

It is an ongoing project, a commitment, a daily obligation.

Just as most of us bathe, brush our teeth, eat and work, so should we parent.

A child support check mailed monthly does not a parent make.

Daily e-mails are not enough.

Children appreciate feeling that their parent is with them in some way.

If you cannot speak with your child every day, you may still play a role in their daily life.

This book was written to provide ideas and suggestions as well as thought-provoking considerations that any "long distance" parent would appreciate.

Following the suggestions in this workbook will help your child feel confident that you are always there for him or her. Please feel free to personalize this workbook by making notes and comments in the blank spaces. Note what is especially important to you. Add your own suggestions. The more you can personalize this book to your own individual situation, the more it will help you shorten the distance.

Please read on…

Predictability

Children need predictability and stability.

They take pride in knowing their parents' patterns, likes, dislikes and little idiosyncrasies; this is a comfort to them. Starting a ritual is a simple process.

Choose one of these to get started, or start something that is unique only to you.

- Make regular phone calls, like every Sunday at 11 am and Wednesdays at 7 pm
- Take responsibility for the yearly Halloween costume
- Send something green on St. Patrick's Day
- Purchase the new "favorite team" shirt for both of you each spring or fall
- Choose greeting cards with a common theme like rainbows or butterflies
- Go to a favorite spot during each visit
- Purchase the annual soccer or ballet shoes

- Always show up with the most current teen magazine
- Listen to the same radio show in the car or a favorite sing-a-long CD

Children look forward to their time with you, it is very important to them. Therefore, first and foremost, ***never*** cancel or drastically change a visitation time or arrangement unless ***absolutely*** necessary. Never be excessively late, making them or their caretakers wait for your arrival. Their feelings are easily hurt, and they don't understand jobs or traffic. Thirty minutes is a long time for a child waiting with anticipation.

Medical Care

Children get sick, and frequently they go to the doctor. They are required to be immunized and receive physicals. Attempt to assist and be aware of the time and expense associated with office visits and prescriptions beyond what insurance pays.

Do you have the information required if they need to check into a hospital? Who is their insurance provider? What is the policy number? This is important to know in the event of an accident or injury while in your care.

Do you know your child's blood type?

Does she/he have allergies?

Do you have a copy of immunization records and dates?

When was the last tetanus shot?

Do you maintain a list of medications taken in the past?

Do you know his/her doctor's and dentist's name, address and phone number?

If at all possible, both parents should establish a presence with the pediatrician. This is not to say that both should go to the routine visits, but instead alternate. While visiting the child in his hometown, perhaps physicals or allergy shots may be scheduled during your time with them.

Heating pads, ice packs, thermometers, bandages, ipecac and humidifiers are good items things to have on hand when the child stays in your home. If you have daughters ages ten through seventeen, be sure to keep sanitary napkins and tampons in the bathroom along with an over the counter menstrual cramp pain reliever.

Their Home

Regardless of how your child got so far away from you, it is crucial that you do not harbor any resentment towards his or her hometown.

Think back to when you were a child and how important your sense of connection was. For instance, were there special places you would go? Were you proud of your school team, colors or slogan?

You may hate the fact that your child lives across the country. You may detest small towns or large cities and despise the weather there. But this is your child's home. This is the place where she/he is growing up. This is where his/her friends live. Favorite activities usually take place there. While you may abhor the snow, they may love to toboggan and ice skate.

It is what children come to know as home and comfort.

Do your best to enjoy it with them.

Learn your way around, so that you may attend some of the functions the children participate in. Downtown, parades, famous sights, parks, etc. are all good choices. Get familiar with a hotel near their residence so when you visit they can easily hang out with you, and possibly with their friends, too. A map can be obtained from the car rental company or the internet.

Subscribe to the child's hometown community mailing list. The City Parks and Recreation department or the local public library usually distributes newsletters. You can use this information along with news you receive from their school to determine the best dates for hometown visits. Imagine the child performing in a choir concert the same week as the town centennial parade and Fall Harvest Festival. This provides activities to do when you are visiting and creates pleasant memories.

Doing things together gives your child a chance to show you off to anyone she/he meets while you are out and about. The opportunity to share his/her surroundings with you means a lot to them, such as experiencing the route your child walks to school each day, enjoying the park where they play, or going to the local public pool where they spend their summer days.

A child who is always reminded that your place of residence is in a better location begins to experience shame and failure at something beyond his/her control. Children may feel that you do not care or may think you don't want to hear about their involvement in activities around town.

Communication starts to dwindle as they get more active in their community. Visits in their hometown are not the time to bring other adults along, nor to go shopping or sightseeing alone or with your friends. Remember that your child lives here and has probably seen and done it all before. This is not your vacation; it is time to be spent bonding and getting to know your child, his/her life and surroundings.

This is also not the time to visit people you know in the area unless they have something in common with your child. Seek out only those adults with compatible children who might play with your son or daughter for a period of time, or those with such things as a swimming pool or trampoline which the two of you can enjoy. Choose only places, people and things that foster you and your child's interaction together. Focus on the children and their interests.

Celebrate their life! Every community has something to offer, so try to learn about the area and enjoy. Avoiding involvement in their life is sacrificing a small piece of them.

Transportation

The issue of transportation between the child's two residences is a big one.

Whether one parent travels with the child back and forth, or the child takes a train, plane or bus, there is much stress involved for all parties. Considerations and concerns of time, expense, safety and weather are never-ending.

Will the child experience air sickness? Will he/she be afraid to fly or travel alone? Is it safe? What if there's a mechanical breakdown?

During winter breaks and summertime there are thousands of children (referred to as unaccompanied minors) traveling on airlines and buses.

Being a retired airline employee, I can address air travel for children.

Airline staff is highly proficient in handling these young passengers. When making an airline reservation for someone under fifteen years old, be absolutely sure the airline understands that the passenger will be an unaccompanied minor. The reservation will be documented as such for personnel both in the departure and in the arrival cities. The airline must know who is dropping the child off at the airport and who will be picking the child up at his or her destination. Name, address and phone number of both parties will be needed. Identification will be necessary. Once in flight, changes are not allowed. If the specified person cannot pick the child up at the destination, call the reservation center of the airline immediately and ask to speak to a supervisor or, better yet, go to your city airport in person. Airline personnel can then verify your identification and contact the arrival airport with explicit instructions. Many airports have chaperoned areas behind ticket counters to use as a lounge for unaccompanied minors. The lounges are available if children have connecting flights or flight delays with twenty or more minutes of waiting time, or if the person responsible for retrieving the child at the destination has been delayed. The lounges usually provide snacks, TV, games and books.

In the event of bad weather or aircraft maintenance, a plane may be diverted to another city. Rest assured that the unaccompanied minors are always a priority. They will be fed and taken to a hotel.

If overnight arrangements are necessary, the child is assigned to stay with airline personnel such as a flight attendant until he/she can be placed back on the plane. However, due to security issues, it is unlikely that anyone including parents, will be allowed to obtain any information over the phone. So if your child is traveling to another city and you hear of an aircraft incident or diversion on the news, do not call the airline and expect them to give you information as to the whereabouts of your child. The airline is not authorized to give out information over the phone about any passenger. This is for passenger safety. You must go in person to an airport, particularly to the same airline your child is traveling on, to receive information. You will be required to give the same information that is detailed in the child's passenger reservation. In most cases, once the child is settled in, the flight crew will have the child contact both his parents.

While in flight:

Quite often kids will begin to dread the trek back and forth. You'll have to creatively entice them to continue.

Some small rituals tend to help:

Plan to have something to do while traveling such as reading.

Have a comic or activity book arrive in the mail the day before the flight. The book will help pass the time on the plane or bus.

Another good idea is to purchase an age-appropriate activity book with different puzzles or word searches and send only a few pages at a time prior to each trip. You can do the same for younger children with a coloring book. Purchase a coloring book to keep at your house and, prior to each trip, copy a couple of pages and mail them along with a small pack of crayons.

Puzzles, word searches, and coloring books can probably be made on a computer as well.

For longer flights of three hours or more, send along five dollars or a headset so she/he can enjoy a movie or listen to music. Most airlines have Disney channels for the smaller children; and listening to music while airborne helps them to sleep, which makes time pass more quickly.

You can consider getting an additional credit card in your children's name. Send the card just before the trip so they can use it on the plane for audio-visual games. Upon their arrival take the card back, promising to mail it the next time they travel.

Another fun idea for younger children is to call them prior to departure and plan a game. Ask the child to count how many people wore red coats or the number of passengers wearing hats? How many pets did they see along the way? They will be anxious to share all the details of their travels with you when they arrive.

The small hand-held electronic games are entertaining. When the child arrives, take the game back, promising to send it again with their next trip. They will continue to look forward to this.

It is important to make sure they are comfortable during their travels. Be sure they have appropriate clothes for the weather that is expected on their trip. See to it that they don't have many items to carry during the trip. Be sure that they are feeling well and up to the trip. It is miserable for anyone to suffer from congestion during a flight or needing of frequent bathroom trips. Always be confident that they are well fed, and have them carry a snack so they will not have to go long without food or drink. Help them learn to alleviate ear pressure or motion sickness symptoms while flying. Sucking or chewing relieves pressure in their ears, so send along gum or hard candy. Explain to them the use of airbags and their location in the seat pockets in front of them.

Siblings

It is a complex situation when your child lives in a household with other children.

It makes no difference if the other children are step-siblings or half-siblings they are simply siblings. Placing a defined term on them does not matter in the grand scheme of things. Those siblings are an integral part of your child's life and those children share so much with your child.

Siblings will leave a huge imprint on your child's memories. They share more with your child on a daily basis than they share with you or perhaps even the custodial parent.

Sharing the same meals, life lessons, watching TV, and maybe sharing clothes are common amongst siblings.

It is important that you are cognizant of the other children. Know who they are, their names, and approximate ages.

Imagine it's a Saturday afternoon and your child is awaiting your arrival to go away for the weekend. Younger siblings don't understand why their brother or sister is leaving for the day or a week. They don't understand why their sibling won't be home for the holiday. Younger ones ask many questions. How is your child to answer? He will need help with this. Is your child made to feel different? Will he be resented later? What about of those that are older or near the same age? Are they resentful that your child gets additional Christmas gifts or escapes Saturday chores? Do the other children have a right to form opinions of the situation or of their impression of you? Of course they do.

While you may not care about what the other children think, believe me, your child does. He/She lives with them and, in many cases, depends on them for many things such as companionship, advice and perhaps even caretaking if the sibling is older.

Consider occasionally taking all the family children along for something as simple as an ice cream treat. An hour or so will make a world of difference to your child. What if you send a little something small to the other kids when you send a small gift to your child? Something as inexpensive as stickers or holiday pencils would work well.

You should be respectful of their relationship and by all means remember: they are children, and children are not rational, and even at times impolite. All children play the game of "my dad can beat up your dad."

Be aware that when doing things with your child, other children are at home. For instance, do not give a child a scary video game or tiny Legos if there are younger children in the household. Custodial parents are responsible for all of the children in the home.

The offending item could be taken away from your child. The child may see one parent taking another parent's gift away and develop resentment, resulting in major problems later down the road. Incorporate polite care and concern into conversations with your child about the other residents in his household. This will let your child know that you are in tune with his/her lifestyle.

Remember, the shoe could be on the other foot. Consider an opposite scenario. Does the stepparent in your child's home have an ex-spouse who visits the siblings? If so, how does that ex-spouse refer to and treat your child? How does your child feel when the others are away and he/she is the odd man out? How would your child feel if she/she simply watched television or played Nintendo all day during your visits while siblings were taken to the city on a shopping spree or to the amusement park with their parents?

Kids talk, compare, and they squeal with excitement. It just happens. Make the best of the whole situation. When you visit with your child, try to participate in his/her entire life. Denying any part of your child's environment, family, or life in general denies a part of the child.

    Work at keeping resentment of others and of themselves at bay.

The Stepparent

Nobody said you have to like the stepparent. In most cases, the decision you and your ex-spouse made to go your separate ways came before the stepparent did. Any person that commits to a relationship that includes responsibility for a child is to be respected. This person chose your ex-spouse just as you did at one time, and they apparently were aware that they'd be a part of your child's life as well. There are several things to keep in mind, whether you like it or not.

The stepparent married to or living with your ex-spouse takes on more than meets the eye. He/She helps to provide a roof over your child's head, food on the table, heat in the winter and cool in the summer. The everyday things such as shampoo, soap, toothpaste, dishwashing and laundry detergent, water, and electricity are their reality, and don't forget HOMEWORK.

All of this is in addition to what they would normally spend or do if your child wasn't living there. One would say that these are the items to which child support payments should be directed. This is true, but have you thought about any of the following?

All children are restricted from school if they have lice, measles or pink eye, so who is taking the days off work to help out? If you are not in town for these things, then how do they get done?

Appointments: doctor, dentist, orthodontist, and guitar lessons all require transportation. Who takes the time from work to retrieve the child from school or daycare and sits through the appointments with them? Prescriptions also need to be picked up.

Who takes and picks the child up from: school, jobs, friends' houses, church outings, school field trips, sports, band practices, or the mall?

Calls: Which parent handles forgotten lunches, homework, picking up a sick child, trouble at school or at part-time jobs?

Embarrassment: Who is the one embarrassed when the child acts inappropriately at school, in the grocery or department store, or at a restaurant, or if he/she hosts a wild party at the house?

Attendance: Who, after working all day, goes to school functions and sports events in the evening, parent-teacher conferences, book and science fairs or band/choir concerts?

Shopping: A parent must purchase party and school supplies, Scout treats, new shoes, spikes for football, ballet shoes, science projects, and teachers' gifts.

Entertainment: Who is the one most likely to host the following: birthday and pool parties, sleepovers, graduation open houses, Brownie or scout meetings, or gatherings prior to dances? Who provides food, cake, decorations, and clean-up?

Privacy: How much quiet time do you have either alone or as a couple? Custodial parents don't attend many happy hours when children are at home, and they sit through many PG rated movies with the children.

Babysitters: Do you assist with babysitting expenses when the custodial parent wants a night out? You probably would if you were still together!

Illness: If children are sick in the middle of the night, who misses work when a child is too ill to go to school or daycare?

What about the wear and tear on household items?

Who covers primary insurance for medical, dental, vision, home or the car?

And there is not a day that goes by that a custodial parent/stepparent doesn't stick their hand in their pocket for any of the following: lunch money, school pictures, teacher and coach gifts, friends' birthdays, school supplies, sporting events, any type of lessons, snacks, weekly reader and book orders, fundraisers, dances, and so on.

The stepparent is part of your child's life and influences him/her as well. Their stories and the lessons they teach stay with the child every bit as much as what you contribute.

It is a good idea to help the child remember the stepparent at Christmas, Mother's or Father's Day, and even birthdays.

The remembrance doesn't have to be anything extravagant; just a little something from the child to show appreciation. This lets stepparents know that you and the child appreciate them and that you acknowledge all they do on a daily basis for your child or children. Extend gratitude in some fashion as acknowledgment of your child's safety and provisions. It certainly makes life nicer for everyone concerned. You don't have to be friends, and the stepparent doesn't have to like you or the little gift, but your child sees the attempted respect. There are many stepparents raising children on a daily basis, keeping them safe and sound for many years, and yet both the biological parent and the child take it for granted. It is the biological parents' obligation to their children that they choose and respect partners to assist them with their upbringing. If the stepparent is doing the best they can, then acknowledge it. If the stepparent doesn't respect you, ignore it.

Child-rearing is exhausting. We all get cranky and say things we shouldn't or don't mean. Unless you are helping out a full fifty percent, the custodial parent and his/her significant other may resent the fact that you only occasionally do your part.

Get over it, and get used to it.

You know the truth. You are the parent, and that will never change. Your relationship is with your child.

You are teaching the child to be a better person by respecting the stepparent or at least the stepparent's efforts. Making sure the child is polite, respectful and treats the stepparent with gratitude will help both the child (and the stepparent) to see what a good person you are. We need to set examples for children to emulate when they grow up. With this behavior, hopefully, the child will grow up and choose to be just like you.

Remember:

You can't expect everything to be the custodial parent's duty.

Forget the response, "She wanted custody, so she can do it all."

Had the two of you stayed together, fifty percent of everything would have been your responsibility. The stepparent is simply picking up the slack in your stead. Be glad that the child has someone in his/her life to do these things.

COMMUNICATION

AND

VISITATION

Toddlers

When you can't be with your child often, remember this: what does any child want, need and deserve?

All little ones need caressing, dependability, consistency and frequency. To put it simply, children need a routine. In fact, comfort and stability is a common need in all of us.

When you do have the ability to be with him/her, keep it simple and always the same. Nap time, lunch, dinner and bedtime should be similar in both households.

Frequent and short visits are a major key.

One long weekend each month or every six weeks works better than one week two or three times a year. For very young children, being with them in their city for consecutive daily visits for five hours a day works better than taking them for three full days. It is advisable to take them home to sleep, as this isn't quite as exhausting or disruptive to the sleep patterns of a small child.

Watching the same video or listening to the same song over and over again is a way of life for little ones. Children learn through repetition. Albeit nerve wracking to adults, there is something about that jingle or those characters that appeals to your child. It is important to respect that and, oh, the laughs you'll get from this when he/she is older!

When visits are at your residence, keep things such as toys and highchairs in the same spot. Constant change can cause anyone to become frustrated and cranky, regardless of age.

Quiet and simple are the keys to loving moments.

Unfamiliar faces, places, smells, animals, noises and food tend to stress youngsters, making them not want to return. This sometimes results in stomachaches, diarrhea, and other symptoms. Extreme weather changes add to discomfort as well. People keep their home thermostats at different temperatures, and this can tend to disrupt sleep patterns.

It is tempting to want to spoil children and want to expose them to all the great things in life, such as a trip to Sea World or Disneyland. However, prior to five years of age, it is doubtful they will remember the experience, but their emotions will remember the stress.

People think they remember at a young age, but it is more likely that, over time, they hear the story repeated and see the pictures enough to believe that they remember. In actuality, all they really know is that they were there. Not until children become adults will they appreciate your efforts, so save the money and frustration.

You may recall that children have wonderful imaginations, which may include imaginary friends. You should honor and enjoy this.

It is not imperative at this age to constantly expose them to other children. Doing so may actually hinder their immune system and create behavioral issues.

It is not necessary that they always interact with their cousins or neighbors at three years old.

What they need at this age is your undivided attention.

Try any of these loving forms of bonding:

- Play make believe on the floor with trucks or stuffed animals
- Place the child in your lap and read a story
- Watch a video together
- Sing nursery rhymes
- Give warm baths and play in the water
- Go for a walk
- Gently roll a ball back and forth

Simple foods and comfortable clothing while in your care are essential, so always have plenty on hand.

An afternoon of sitting in your lap watching Barney or a Disney movie is much better for two and three year olds than a day at the circus anytime.

These moments create attachments that cannot be matched.

Preschooler Communication

This is the age that the true personality and wonderful ideas begin to develop.

A lot of questions will be asked. Fears begin to form.

Vocabulary becomes strong.

This point is between the baby stage and a child, and they will waiver back and forth between these two phases of their life.

Constant contact with them is necessary.

They will want to try new things, only to become scared at the last minute.

They will like a particular food today but not tomorrow.

They have very short attention spans.

They cannot control their emotions or their bodily functions; when they say they need to go potty, it means right now.

Telling a child in advance about an exciting event such as an upcoming trip or holiday is almost torture for them. By the time that event takes place, they will have gotten so worked up about it that everyone involved will quickly become miserable and exhausted.

Preschoolers cannot make decisions and shouldn't be burdened with having to try.

Don't ask them where they want to go to eat or on vacation, or even what they want for Christmas. You will know all of these things by spending time with them.

At four and five years old, children can begin speaking on the phone but expect only a very few words. Only obvious conversation is best; avoid yes or no questions.

Try asking these:

- What are you doing right now?
- Is it sunny or raining at your house?
- What did you watch on TV today?
- What did you do in preschool today?
- What did you have for lunch/dinner?
- What color shirt are you wearing today?

Tell the child you are thinking of him/her right now and that you wanted to say, "I love you and miss you" and will call again or visit soon. Phone calls two or three times a week help the child with dialogue and phone etiquette. He/She will begin to look forward to your conversations.

Kids this age love to receive mail.

Cards or letters must be very simple, and you don't even need to write anything because they can't read much more than their name.

Preschoolers love stickers and pictures to color, but just one or two in an envelope will suffice. If you send a whole package of stickers, they will be stuck all over the house.

Give them one big sticker to apply to their favorite sweatshirt, and they are good to go. One picture to color provides them with ten minutes of enjoyment.

Print their name in big letters on the envelope with your name in the return address.

Something like this will make their day. Buy one package of stickers so you can send a few in the mail once a week for a couple of months.

This fun activity between the two of you will provide a topic of discussion for the next call.

One picture of just you or of the two of you together sent in an envelope every six to eight months gives them a remembrance and something to show off at school during sharing time. But a single photo will do since they do not appreciate a scrapbook at this age.

Before you know it, a scrapbook in the hands of a preschooler will become exactly that.... scrap!

Preschooler Activities

When with the child, again, keep things easy. Keep food, clothing and activities casual.

Most children this age have lots of energy and should be kept busy, with down time in between to re-charge.

While in your care, energy-releasing activity can include:

- Going to the park to play on swings, slides and jungle gyms
- Swimming
- Riding bikes or rollerblading
- Walking the dog
- Washing the car
- Tossing a soft squishy style ball
- Playing at fast-food places' activity centers

Quiet-time activities to do together:

- Coloring
- Flash cards
- Puzzles
- Playing an age-appropriate card game or dominoes
- Reading a story out loud
- Playing beauty shop and brushing each other's hair
- Polishing little girls' nails
- Beginning to learn a foreign language

Four and five year olds need to feel comfortable in your home.

They need signs that they live there:

- Plastic magnetic alphabet letters on your refrigerator
- Hand-drawn pictures and schoolwork displayed
- Pictures of the child in view

- Their favorite snacks and drinks in the refrigerator or cabinets
- Child-like objects as well as additional change of clothes and shoes in their room
- Toys, books and videos available to them in an obvious place

Things you can do:

- Contact the preschool or kindergarten with your name, address and phone number.
- Request a copy of scheduled activities.
- Plan to chaperone or attend one of their scheduled activities. If you are unable to attend, at least you will be in the know and can discuss the activities with your child.
- Be sure to find out about school pictures and make an effort to purchase or share the expense with the other parent. Call to remind the child of picture day so they are prepared.

- Find out what the school policy is for treats. Perhaps you could mail a box of pencils or a package of suckers for your child's birthday.
- If your little one is involved with a sport or music lessons, for instance write or call the coach or instructor for a list of games or concerts.
- If you cannot attend these events perhaps you could send a card or flowers as a "good luck" wish.
- If the event can be recorded, perhaps someone would make a copy for you. You can send a blank DVD and offer to pay for a copy of the video and the mailing expense or the other person could download it and send it to you via the internet. You and your child can watch it together at a later date.
- By all means, plan a vacation day or sick day if necessary and attend something each and every school year.

- If nothing else, at least go to the school, meet the teacher and see their classroom. Kids take great pride in this.
- Make an effort to know the teachers'/coaches' names and the name of at least one of your child's friends to use in conversation.
- If the child has a family pet, find out the name and use it. Ask with care and concern about their pets, hobbies, friends and siblings.
- If you are in the area where the child resides, make an attempt to share in the doctor, dental and optometrist visits.

You can do the following when you are in the area, or you can do these things while they are with you in your town:

- Take them for a haircut.
- Have their eyes checked. (There are optometrists and hairdressers everywhere.)

- Shop for clothes, shoes, coats. Children outgrow these things fast.
- Provide a few necessary school or sporting supplies.
- Shop for upcoming events in their life, such as a costume for Halloween.
- Choose a teacher's gift to be offered at Christmas or at the end of the school year.
- Schedule annual sport or school physicals. If necessary, public sites are set up in cities for immunizations. These are usually less expensive and time-consuming than a visit to a doctor.

While the above-mentioned things are not always fun and while you may send monetary support for these things, remember…….

It is not a matter of child support;
It is a matter of child rearing.
This is what parents should do for their children.

Kindergarten through 2nd Grade Activities

Full-time activity in school is a way of life for children in these grades. Many are in sports, scouts, music lessons, and other activities.

They have many people in their lives and they begin to have heroes.

These could be pop stars, cartoon super heroes or TV characters.

Children this age are showing signs of interest and in many cases, this is an indication of interests they will carry through the rest of their lives.

Their hobbies could be art, reading, music, sports, science, fashion, or any number of things. When you see their enthusiasm begin to spark, encourage them.

Now is the time to take them to their first museum, movie, concert, play, circus, parade and other events.

At eight years old children begin learning how to operate DVD or CD-players and become amazingly independent if allowed to do so.

Discover their interest and help to show them the proper way to develop it.

Nothing should be forced upon them.

Nobody ever died because they quit piano lessons or soccer.

Encourage them to try and if they don't enjoy something, let it go.

It would be wise to encourage any child who has the capability to be active and outdoors as much as possible. Promoting physical activity is easy at this age. If a child gets caught up sitting indoors at a computer, watching TV or playing video games all day, it gets harder to encourage physical activity later.

Things to do at this age:

- Zoo
- Museums
- Amusement parks
- Art centers
- Concerts
- Hiking
- Charitable walks
- Wildlife centers
- SeaWorld
- Fishing
- Camping
- ATV riding
- Motocross
- Scouts
- Church outings
- Roller blading or skating
- Snow and water skiing

- Golfing
- Go-carts
- Trampolines
- Work at charity events or fundraisers
- Foreign language
- Tours of the fire and police stations
- Library
- Arts and crafts sessions
- Swimming
- Sewing
- Painting
- Board and card games
- Cooking or baking
- Gardening

Take advantage of all the freebie activities the city has to offer. Whether in your own town or where your child lives, check out the Sunday paper for area activities.

Take advantage of the local library to research the city's parks and recreation services and see what they have to offer.

Your local crafts store or teachers' supply store will have oodles of age-appropriate inexpensive activities.

TV as well as video and electronic games should be reserved for resting times.

Daily Reminders

Encouraging your child to care about or attend to something each day provides the child with a constant connection to you and expands their personal interests. The next time the two of you are together, you might choose one of the following items to work with:

- Caring for a potted plant
- Airplane, car, truck, or boat, model making, which you proudly display in your home upon completion
- An ongoing online chess game
- A diary or journal purchased by you
- A series of books to read
- A science project to tend to daily
- A musical instrument to practice
- A small pet (fish, bird, lizard, gerbil) to be fed daily, with bowls and/or cage cleaned weekly. You should provide for expenses and make the daily reminders.

Teaching the child to care for an animal is as much benefit to the child as it is to the animal. As a matter of fact, it benefits our whole society.

Something as mentioned above, along with regular phone calls, frequent letters, postcards or e-mails will keep the two of you close.

Preteens Ages 9-13 Activities and Interests

The preteen period is probably one of the most important times in everyone's life since it signifies transition from childhood to teenager.

This age group tries to identify who they think they want to be. This is a genuine time for you as well. You will find yourself thinking, "Who are you, and what have you done with my little girl/boy?"

This is where life-long friendships can begin; these can be beneficial or disastrous. This is when they become defined by the "crowd."

Regardless of who your child is, right now she/he is trying to define how to be popular and accepted.

It is VERY important to them.

Nobody wants to be a nerd or an outcast. They want to be accepted and they need your help and guidance during this critical time.

The following lists are usually of interest to kids of this age frame:

Preteen girls' interests:

- Shopping, especially at the mall
- Clothes, jewelry, fashion, shoes
- Personal items, i.e., hair, makeup and nail polish
- Preteen magazines: Tiger Beat, BOP
- Books
- Movies and Videos
- Posters
- Music
- MTV and teen-related programs
- Dance, gymnastics and sports

Things preteen girls like to do:

- Sporting events
- Board games or cards
- Science exhibits or events

- Musical concerts
- Crafts
- Instruction, i.e., music, karate, archery
- Car repair and maintenance
- Building or assembly
- Hunting, fishing, camping
- Household chores
- Cooking or baking

Preteen boys' interests:

- Transportation: stock cars, bikes, scooters, skateboards, surfboards, inline skates, motorcycles, go-carts, boats, etc.
- Electronics
- Movies
- Books or magazines pertaining to their interests
- Music and Instruments
- Collections - rocks, hot wheels cars, baseball cards, etc.

- Sports - Team or individual
- Action, sports, cartoon or TV heroes
- Body building
- Crafts or hobbies such as drawing, painting, hunting, camping, and building structures or engines
- Science and chemistry
- Animals
- Magic
- Food

Things preteen boys like to do:

- Shopping, especially at the mall
- Any form of skating
- Movies
- Animals
- Horseback riding
- Music - listening, learning to play, singing
- Live dance productions

- Cooking or baking
- Sporting events
- Reading
- Theatre

Boys and girls this age love macaroni & cheese, grilled cheese, quesadillas, sandwiches, oatmeal, cereal, soup, hot dogs, popcorn, nachos, salads, wings, cookies and pizza. Preteens like practically any foods that are ready-made and microwaveable. This is the time to begin advising them on the hows and whys of proper nutrition and exercise. It is also an excellent opportunity to explain kitchen safety, along with teaching them how to cook small, light meals.

Summer Visits

How to spend you time in the summer is a hard thing to decide.

Remember, the lazy days of summer when you were their age?

Sleeping late, watching cartoons in the morning, running about the neighborhood with friends, swimming, sleepovers, camp and sports were enticing options.

Hopefully, your child will have someone to pal around with where you live.

Maybe you can register him/her for a sports or summer program in your area. This is an excellent way for children to make friends.

There is such a period of adjustment for the child upon arrival and then readjustment to being back at home again.

Not many children like to get back home to their friends and hear about all the fun they missed. Why tear them away from their other family and friends only to leave them with a sitter at your residence during visits? Extended periods of visitation are hard on a child.

Have you never felt homesick? A child usually won't let anyone know he/she is uncomfortable for fear of hurting your feelings.

Short visits possibly twice during the summer are so much easier for everyone. Two or three weeks at the beginning of summer and perhaps another week or two before school resumes works very well.

Planning a week-long vacation near their place of residence or in another state very nearby is fun. You can pick them up or make arrangements for them to meet you there. Using this method, children can enjoy downtime at home, vacation time with you as well as vacation time with their other family and maybe even with grandparents. They would also have time for bible school, band camp, or even a short season of baseball or softball.

Would you want to "live" somewhere else longer than three weeks? They say it takes that period of time to form a habit. Must the child repeatedly start all over? What about the family conditions? If there are other children in the primary home, is this hard on your child as well as on the siblings? This is a huge issue for most families. The determining factor in the decision should be what is good for the child, not what works best for vacation time or for the extended family, such as grandparents.

Extra Curricular Activities

Extra curricular activities require time and money.

Think back to when you were young. There are physicals, uniforms, shoes, equipment, lessons, instruments, transportation to get to practice, pictures and gifts for coaches and instructors.

School costs include raffles, pizza parties, money for trophies, lunches, field trips, book fairs and science projects. They will be invited to attend birthday parties and bring gifts. Schools are always encouraging fundraisers and asking children to sell items. School activities always require chaperones. Contact instructors or coaches, get the schedule of activities and find a way to contribute or to attend some of the functions.

If you can't attend, then you could call the day before to wish them good luck or to say, "Have fun."

Always phone again the day after to discuss their evening or event, and encourage pictures or video when possible.

Social Activities

You may remember those simple pleasures in your youth, like having money to hang out at the mall, for lunch out with friends, to buy movie tickets, or to pay entrance fees to school and sporting functions.

Who will cover all of these expenses? How will the child be taught the value of a dollar? Will your son or daughter receive a weekly allowance? Will you child be encouraged to seek employment?

If so, will the custodial parent be solely responsible for paying the allowance or for the transportation to and from the child's job? Will the employment hinder their studies or their ability to enjoy high school activities?

Perhaps they can save money through the summer, which can later be distributed throughout the following school year.

These lessons about time and money management require the equal responsibility of both parents.

Teens Ages 14-17

Be prepared!

This may be the hardest time for you.

Remember your high school days? Probably they consisted of school work, homework, projects, sports, band, dances, hanging out and parties. Your child may not have time for you. It would be the same if they lived with you; this is normal and natural. Do not be offended.

This is also the time they're most likely to get into trouble.

Be their parent, not their friend. Prepare them for adulthood and responsibility. Everyone pays consequences, so it's better to do that now rather than later in life.

Your conversations and time together may not be very fun or pleasant. Talks with them may be very serious and produce anger. If your child doesn't get into some kind of trouble or is never angry with the other parent or an authority figure at any time, for any reason, then you don't know your child or what is really going on.

They will most likely try smoking, alcohol, drugs, sex, avoid curfews, get into fights, talk back, steal, lie, experience sibling rivalry, rebel, be grounded, get expelled, or worse. Their grades may begin to slip. Their interests will change. So may their friends.

There are important social events during this time. Dances and recitals requiring new clothes or uniforms, money for tickets, flowers, pictures, dinner, and maybe even a limo shared expense. Girls will need hair and nail appointments, shoes, and new clothes. Boys need guidance with tuxedos, dating, and dinner protocol.

It is your obligation to be aware of these very important times in their lives. What can you do to help?

There are significant competitions coming up, many of which may be useful toward acquiring scholarships. They may be sports related, art, yearbook and writing, band

and choir, speech and debate, photography or academic, to name a few. You will want to do your best to try to attend any of these contests.

There are post-high school education choices to begin to consider, which is time-consuming. Writing and research is needed. Jump in now, make the calls, have information sent out to both homes, and review all of it together.

Very important academic studies at this time include papers and stories to write, research to do, languages to study, heavy-duty homework, and college preparatory tests to schedule and prepare for.

Where can you step in?

Can you pick up the Cliff Notes or see a movie to better associate yourself with the subjects they are studying? Are you able to send them literature about a place or activity you have experienced? Can you do the preliminary research on the internet or at the library? Share your own experiences with them to help during this time.

Kids ages 14-17 may become interested in the following:

- Writing
- History
- Photography
- Genealogy
- Fashion
- Art
- Career choices
- Love interests

Find out what their hot button is and guide them. Expose them to whatever you can and most importantly, be open minded. Your idea of art, fashion, music, or poetry, will probably not be the same as theirs.

Get in there and do your part; this may be the last time you can.

After graduation, your young adult could go off to college, work, or enter the military. Maybe they'll get married or move to another state or country. You may not have the opportunity to be of assistance or offer guidance again. By this time, our teachings just start to become old stories.

When Your Teen Comes to Your Home

When your teen comes to visit, you probably feel that you only have a small amount of time with them, so you avoid confrontations.

You don't want to say "no." You don't want to deny them the opportunity to watch an "R" rated movie just this once and besides, you want to see the movie as well. You want to stay up and play chess, which overrides their usual bedtime. You find them playing a violent video game that you aren't comfortable with, yet you let it slide.

You have to leave them at home alone occasionally and realize you have no parental controls on the computer or cable TV. You notice a few cigarettes missing and give them the benefit of the doubt. After they return home you receive a $200 long-distance phone bill with numerous calls they made to their friends, a late statement from the video store and cable statements indicating pay per view adult movies were ordered. Yet you say nothing.

This is all quite understandable. The last thing you wish to do is complain about having them stay with you. But what about the child?

Do they go back and brag to their friends and siblings? You bet they do.

Does the custodial parent now have issues because of your visitation?

Will their teachers and other parents hear the stories?

Will your child now be considered a bad influence to others? What about his relationship with the other children in his/her home?

When you visit your child, will the parents of his/her playmates be reluctant to let their children go along with you?

Will the child's teacher make comments that they notice a difference in his/her behavior after visiting with the non-custodial parent? Does this eventually make things harder for the child in some manner? Are they tired and cranky upon their return or are they disruptive in school? Does the child truly feel resentment because things are so different? Does he/she have less respect for you by thinking that you are gullible, a pushover, or irresponsible? As the child matures, will she/he look back and see that you wouldn't have made a good custodial parent?

Children feel more confident, stable and safe if their life is consistent. If you are only going to be with the child a short amount of time, it is certainly easier for you to adjust than it is for the child.

If your child is going to spend extended amounts of time at your home and you must leave them occasionally, it is relatively simple to appoint parental controls on the TV and computers. Even movie theatres now have restrictions.

It is easier to be tough and ease up later than it is to be easy and then toughen up.

When your child is visiting, keep your lifestyle age-appropriate. If anything comes up that you are unsure of, simply ask someone else in his/her life. It will be appreciated.

The custodial parent does not set all the rules.

Age-appropriate activities at the proper times are just plain good common sense.

You are the parent first, and the friend second.

Money

Giving children a lot of money is giving them a dangerous toy.

Children known to have money are never really sure who their friends are, and they are usually taken advantage of.

When the money is no longer there, amazingly, neither are many of their friends. This causes humiliation to a child, depleting their dignity and self-esteem. What will they do next to be "top dog"?

Too much money robs them of the opportunity to earn it and the thrill of accomplishment, deteriorating their pride, integrity and self-respect.

It lessens goal-setting qualities.

It is a proven fact that people without goals become bored and eventually boring to others. Once a person becomes boring, they eventually become lonely. Loneliness can lead to depression, drugs and alcohol.

Very few of us respect people who have everything handed to them. Is this the way you want your child to be perceived by others?

Do you want them to become unable to support and care for themselves and their future families?

Giving large amounts of money at holidays or birthdays is the easy way out. While few children refuse money thrown their way, deep inside they know that you haven't taken the time to shop with them or for them. They learn quickly that you don't know them well enough to be aware of their interests, sizes, etc.

When sending a child a check or money, especially prior to learning to drive, who takes the child to the bank and shopping? Is he/she actually bonding with another instead of enjoying a birthday gift from you? What does the child remember and enjoy more, the check from you or the experience and time spent at the mall with someone else?

It is acceptable in our society for grandparents to give money, because grandparents are now considered "way out of touch." So, save check-writing for your grand parenting days.

Enough cash to get through one evening is all the money a child should have on hand.

A fast-food meal, a movie, or several games at the video arcade can equal $20 or more easily. That amount blown over one weekend is plenty. The rest of the time they can do free or low-cost things, like go to a friend's house, shoot pool, play games, swim, enjoy rented movies, and toss the football at the park.

School lunches range from $2 on campus to $4.50 for fast food, which totals approximately $20 per week.

Household's and neighbors' odd jobs could be a source of income if more money is needed for something special.

Children from age 14 can handle a little responsibility such as babysitting, light housework, yard work, car washing, raking or shoveling. Eventually, this age group could get a part time job. If this theory of money in exchange for work is not implied, how will your child make it in our society?

Gift money from others, such as grandparents, should be used constructively. Pick something that the money will be used for and spend it in a timely manner; otherwise, before you know it, your child has wasted it all on junk food or other things you don't want to know about.

Imagine the pride they will exude when they know they have purchased that car, new tires or guitar with their own money. Even if they only contribute half, they will increase their pride and self-awareness ten-fold.

Regardless of how much money you have, if you set a good example for them when they're youngsters, most likely they will do very well in life. Don't we ultimately want them to be happy with their lives and to be sure they have it better, easier and have more than we did?

Isn't that a parent's goal?

Teaching children the value of money and the ability to manage it is one of the most important gifts you can give to your child. This lesson will stay with them for a lifetime and save them anguish and hardship in their future.

Know the Facts

You need to know the facts about childhood from ages twelve through seventeen and, as stated throughout this book, you are their parent first and their friend second.

Teenagers can be hard to live with, so sibling rivalry is normal and natural. Whether those other children in the household are stepsisters and stepbrothers, natural siblings or half siblings, there will be some friction.

Disagreements on clothes, chores, privileges, and who watches what on TV, are common.

If you have brothers and sisters, do you remember these incidents?

Since children in the same household typically fight, this doesn't always mean that one child is being treated unfairly.

Teenage rebellion is normal and natural. Find out the facts. Children go through this, especially those from divorced homes.

If it seems your child is frequently grounded, get both sides of the story. Speak with the parent or stepparent to find out why.

Your child's excuse may be, "I came home a *little* late Saturday night."

You may find out that late was 1 hour and 45 minutes late, and it was the third time this month!

There isn't a child around that feels like they have been justifiably grounded!

You can always go a step or two further; while you may not be able to get along with your ex, there is no reason why you can't occasionally visit with other people that your child associates with.

I am not advocating that you get others involved in your communication issues. Simply calling your child's drum instructor to find out how he or she is doing is certainly appropriate. Choose one of your child's best friends and visit with their parents. It is an appreciated gesture to phone them to say how much you appreciate all the driving they do for the kids who attend ballet lessons or Boy Scouts. You can mention the fact that your son or daughter seems to be grounded all the time and that you hope it is not affecting their child as well. See what they have to offer as opinions; you may get an earful.

You should be contacting the child's football coach, teachers, doctor, scout leader, etc. on a regular basis.

See if there is anything you can do to help, and always leave your name and number for emergencies. Somebody will contact you if they feel that your child is being mistreated in any way.

Discipline is the responsibility of both parents and you can share in that from afar.

Remember helping with the expense of an allowance or their car? These things can always be taken away for inappropriate behavior.

Think your child may be mistreated by the other parent, stepparent or step-sibling? Well, if you are in contact with your child on a regular basis and have always made an effort to be active in his/her social life, then you will know the signs yourself or will be contacted if she/he has been unjustly mistreated.

Regardless of how you feel, do not feed the parental rebellion. If the child is hostile toward the other parent at this time, just listen. Get the whole story from all angles, including from siblings, if possible. Remember, you don't have to live there, and so stated before, teenagers are very hard to live with.

To side with your teen at this time only makes life at home worse for your child. If the she/he recites back to the custodial parent or stepparent any derogatory comments you may have said or agreed to, especially when the parent and child are having a heated debate, this only opens the way for parents or stepparents to unload all their negative thoughts about you. Will the thoughts expressed be true or exaggerated? What does this do to the child? Does he/she feel anger? Does he/she hate all adults at this moment?

When your child complains, listen and tell him you will get all the facts.

This encourages the child to always speak only the truth, thereby avoiding humiliation.

If your child doesn't want you to speak with the other parent, coach or teachers, then chances are something is amiss.

Sometimes children will express hostility towards the other adults in their life because they feel that is what you wish to hear. They believe it is a way to get your attention and to be closer to you and your feelings. This is unhealthy.

Often, if a child is willing to move away from all that he/she loves, such as friends, school, activities, and pets so she/he can live with the other parent, he/she is trying to do one of two things:

1) hurt the custodial parent

2) hurt the non-custodial parent (because in most cases this sets up the non-custodial parent to fail).

After a while, the newness will wear off and the child will want to go back to his/her normal surroundings. This causes the parents and the child to feel as though they failed, and everyone involved will feel bad.

Think long and hard while considering all the facts before such things occur.

Driving

This is the time when they take on the first big challenge in their life: taking responsibility for themselves and the safety of others. This will require serious thought process and negotiation, and the parents must set boundaries.

Discussions need to take place regarding insurance, such as the cost and who will carry the child on which policy. Will the parents pick up the tab or will the child be responsible for part? The child should completely understand how insurance works and know what to do in various situations. What will the child drive? How about the vehicle maintenance? It shouldn't only be the custodial parent's vehicle at risk. If a car is damaged, will there be an increase in premiums, and who will absorb this increase? How will you and/or the child split the cost of any damage? What about breaking the law? Which parent will attend court, and who will pay the cost of violation tickets? Which brave one will teach your child to drive? Will the lesson take place on an automatic or stick shift vehicle?

This is a huge responsibility that should not be left up to one person and is not to be taken lightly or for granted, by either parent or child.

These discussions would take place if both parents lived together. The child stands to learn so much from handling this difficult and important life-altering event correctly. Regardless of where you are; GET INVOLVED!

Decisions and negotiations about expenditures and responsibility should be put in writing by both parents, and the child should be knowledgeable about these decisions.

Senior Year

The senior year in high school is the icing on the cake. It is such a busy and important year of their life. There are senior pictures, class rings, graduation announcements, yearbooks, and on and on. Besides graduation, there is the prom and homecoming, too.

There are many ways to get involved. Contact the counselor's office and be sure to get on the mailing list. Most schools have graduation committees that plan and prepare for graduation week. You can get on their e-mail or newsletter lists.

If you are unable to attend any of the fund-raising or planning sessions, you can certainly send money for one of the products that will be needed. Something as simple as decorative crepe paper may be beneficial.

You may also be able to do something long distance, such as word processing to create flyers to be sent as an e-mail attachment for printing.

Take it from me, most of these committees are made up of the same old, tired parents that have done everything year-round for the last 12 years. They could use some fresh new ideas and another set of helping hands.

Be aware of the dates. Post them on your refrigerator, in your daily planner or on your handheld.

Let the child know that you are involved.

Do they need a haircut before pictures?

Have they picked out a gown for the dance? If so, can you go to your local store and pay for it and have it shipped? Can you have something done online?

Does your son need assistance in selecting his first tuxedo?

Can you call the local florist and pre-pay for boutonnières or corsages needed for dances?

Can you get on the internet or look in the phone book and order the limo six weeks prior? Remember the dinner, tickets and pictures that are also part of this.

Will there be a graduation party and a cake? Can you supply a list of addresses for announcements or perhaps provide the postage?

Consider having flowers sent to your daughter for graduation.

You can be a part of all this from afar.

BIRTHDAYS

AND

HOLIDAYS

Birthdays Ages 1-2-3

Keep it simple! One gift is plenty.

At this age, many children would rather play with the boxes than the gifts.

A Hostess cupcake with candles will suffice and be just as fun and messy.

Cake, gifts, cards, decorations and many guests are not necessary.

Gift ideas:

- Buy clothing
- Establish a savings account or a lockbox so relatives can contribute money or savings bonds for years to come.
- Purchase an insurance policy or IRA in the child's name for future education or down payments for a first home.

Something for their room:

- Pint-size chair
- Pictures
- Crib sheets
- Keepsakes

Begin a collection of:

- Collectible figurines
- Collectible toy cars
- Comic books
- Baseball or basketball cards
- Start a photo album
- Keep a journal about your perspective on life since the date of their birth.
- Establish some sort of storage container for a life long collection of commemorative publications and periodicals. These are published after a historical event such as the World Series, space shuttle launch or the death of an influential/historical individual.

Remember:

- Their gift should be nothing that goes into the mouth or ears.

- Do nothing that would take them away from their normal daily activities, such as naptime.

- Surroundings should be comfortable and familiar; no loud restaurants or the like at this age.

Birthdays Ages 4-17

Kids begin to treat birthdays as holidays and hold them more near and dear to their heart than Thanksgiving or Easter. They tend to make extravagant plans and talk about it for weeks prior. Their plans will change many times before the big day.

It would be wise to arrange for a gift to be delivered to the child's home if you live far away. Talk with your child; if they are having friends over, then having a cake, flowers or balloons delivered would be exciting. Arranging for entertainment such as clowns or magicians would be fun, but certainly check with the adult in charge first.

For teens, parties are not always an option, because adults would be there and ruin everything! Certainly they will expect you to give them something, but they don't necessarily want you around. In most cases, they just want to be with their friends.

For any age, choose a time-frame around the big day to get together and do something special. Something as simple as taking their friends for pizza or a movie usually works really well. A little something wrapped and given just before the outing is nice. A pair of earrings or a really awesome t-shirt at this age is usually appreciated or simply letting them pick out their gift at the mall. An outing with a friend or relative makes for a great day. Spending the day doing just what they like to do is the best present ever.

A word about giving gift certificates to teenagers: Gift certificates are nice for such things as clothes or electronics but, as stated in the money section, someone else will be taking them shopping.

In addition, gift certificates are easily lost or accidentally washed, resulting in nothing and causing the child embarrassment or stress.

Gift suggestions for girls 4-17:

- Jewelry; usually the inexpensive gaudy stuff is best at this age
- Hair accessories
- Teen magazines
- Teen-related books (your librarian or bookstore can make suggestions)
- Movies and videos
- Passes to movies or events that they can attend with their friends
- Posters
- Picture frames
- Clothes (they will let you know where to shop)
- Bath accessories
- Beauty accessories - polish, lotions and makeup
- Stuffed animals
- Music
- Lessons – dance, gymnastics, sports, etc.

Gift suggestions for boys 4-17:

- Transportation - stock cars, bikes, scooters, skateboards, surfboards, inline skates, motorcycles or go-carts
- Electronics - remote control anything
- Books/Movies
- Music and instruments
- Collections - rocks, toy cars, baseball cards, etc.
- Sports - passes, tickets, mitts, bats, etc.
- Action sports or cartoon or TV hero figures
- Magazines pertaining to their interests
- Body-building accessories (teens)
- Crafts or hobbies - art accessories, hunting, camping, building structures or engines
- Science and chemistry items
- Animals or animal interest activities, such as riding lessons
- Magic

Halloween

There are costumes for sale in every town.

Have your child go through flyers like the Sunday newspaper or the store mailers, circle the costumes they like and mail the ads to you.

Your child can tell you what he/she is interested in, and you can purchase the costume or accessories for him/her. This is easily done these days through the internet.

Better yet, come up with a homemade costume that you can add to, such as sending them an old shirt, a hat or a pair of old glasses. Tubes of colored makeup, a set of false eyelashes or plastic fangs can be purchased in grocery stores and easily mailed.

Purchase a Halloween treat bag or plastic pumpkin, or make one yourself. Fill it with goodies, including healthy stuff like apples, pumpkin seeds and trail mix, and send it off to them prior to the big day.

Older kids would enjoy a card and perhaps a pre-packaged bag of their favorite treat to share with their friends and siblings.

By phone or e-mail, explain how to make these cute treats, or you can make the Ghost Pops yourself and send them along in the mail:

Ghost Pop

Tootsie Pops with a Kleenex over the top and rubber band at the "neck". A marker makes the face, and you have a sweet little ghost.

Ghost Toast/Ghost Cookie

Using a piece of toast, cut out a ghost figure with a ghost cookie cutter. If you prefer to use a cookie, you will need to cut the cookie dough, bake and cool before going on to the next step.

Spread with soft cream cheese and use raisins for eyes.

Could you send something to the school for the Halloween party? Older kids get a kick out of fun stuff like Halloween socks, pencils or t-shirts.

It would be great if you could show up and take them trick or treating in their own neighborhood with their friends; however if they have other siblings and it is a family affair, they shouldn't be made to feel like the odd man out or have to choose between you and the siblings. Instead, you can see them sometime close to Halloween and enjoy one of the many Halloween or Fall Harvest-type festivals in town together. You might try something silly such as:

- Bobbing for apples from a bowl or the kitchen sink
- Attending an age-appropriate haunted house is exciting for some children
- There are easy caramel apples kits, now available in the produce section at the grocery store

- Munch on popcorn while watching a Halloween movie

There are a variety of Halloween movies out, and your local video store usually highlights these during the month of October.

For the younger set, there are the classics such as:
- Casper cartoons
- Hocus Pocus
- ET
- The Addams Family
- The Legend of Sleepy Hollow

Original black-and-white Bella Lugosi flicks are interesting for the older children.

This would be a good time to introduce them to trilogies such as Star Wars, Lord of the Rings, Harry Potter or Indiana Jones.

The Harry Potter or Goosebumps Series books are great fun to read out loud.

Together, the two of you can get into the Halloween **'*spirit*'**!

Easter Ages 4-17

Mindful of the religious beliefs and ceremonies, how can you participate?

Will the child need new clothes for church? Maybe you could send your son a tie or a hair barrette for your daughter's new outfit. How about an inexpensive costume bracelet or watch to dress up the occasion?

Start a collection of:

- Alabaster eggs
- Bunny figurines
- Little toy cars

Send one each year, starting a fun tradition.

Here are a few other ideas:

- Obtain a Ziploc disposable container from the grocery store or use a shoebox, and fill it with Easter grass and a few of the child's favorite Easter treats. Time the mailing so it arrives on the Friday or Saturday before Easter. Don't forget the old Easter standards of paddle balls and a bottle of bubbles.

- Instead of the Easter Bunny, do Easter Button (a button exchange). Both you and the children send a button to each other the week of Easter. Each of you maintains your collection in a strange jar or container or glued to a poster board. Show off your collection in your home or office, just because.
- Another cute idea would be to send a package of flower seeds for planting (sunflowers are easy). It is fun and conversational to watch the flowers grow. Ask them to send you pictures of their progress.
- And as always, little girls love to receive bouquets of flowers.
- For older children, use this weekend to set a tradition of deciding on your summer vacation destination. Send a nice Easter card with a couple

summer vacation ideas written inside and include a picture from a magazine of each destination. Also include a self addressed, stamped envelope for the child to return to you indicating his/her choice.

Make a significant impact on the child so that each Easter they are reminded of you in some way.

Thanksgiving

Frankly speaking, most children would say that Thanksgiving is boring.

Even though it goes without being said, I will anyway: Thanksgiving is about being thankful for what we have ... food, family, friends, health and prosperity.

Unless a child has been through terrible hunger or awful medical traumas, most children could care less about these things and take it all for granted. If your child hasn't had extreme life experiences then this after all, is a good thing. My point is that few children would hold it against you if you were not with them on "turkey day" or if you didn't provide them with a turkey dinner. In fact, there are many people who are vegetarians or those that simply don't like turkey!

Make it easy on yourself and those involved. If there are big plans on the other parent's side, then let the child be there and relax with that side of his/her family.

Isn't that what we would all like to do, relax on a holiday? If you live far away, choose another time to be together, avoiding airports, weather delays and expense.

Take it from an ex-airline employee, that first week of December is the best time to travel.

Another option would be to travel to the child's hometown on Thanksgiving Day. The airports are very quiet at that time. It makes more sense quality-wise to be with your child or children on the Friday and Saturday following the holiday, enjoying something you all love to do.

Thanksgiving is the time for shopping bargains and movie premiers. It is also a good time to get to know their friends or visiting cousins, as they are out of school at this time.

Fun activities along with great specials are going on this time of year, such as bowling, ice skating, roller or inline skating, ceramic shops, etc., where you can take a couple of kids for a good time. Having them spend the night at your hotel and swimming in an indoor pool would be awesome, too.

It would probably be best to make advance reservations for any of the previous things mentioned either by telephone or the internet.

If Thanksgiving is the big day for your family and there are many activities for the children, then so be it. An arrangement of alternate years is probably the best way.

Remember that children are sensitive; if you are not going to be with them, always lead them to believe that you have somewhere to go or you have friends to be with. Do not let them think that you are alone for the holidays. This creates feelings of guilt for your child.

Prior to Thanksgiving, if you're not going to be together, ask the younger kids to mail a picture they have colored, a Thanksgiving craft they made, or a recent poem they've written, so you can show it to your family and friends during the Thanksgiving holiday. Share with your kids any compliments received on their project the next time you speak on the phone or in your next e-mail.

If they are older, call them on Thanksgiving Day so each of you can share what you are thankful for and talk about their plans for the upcoming long weekend.

Christmas-type Holidays Ages 1-2-3

Again, as stated previously, the simple things are the best.

Many people, many gifts, and an overload on traditions such as meals and sweets are not necessary.

At this age, many children would rather play with the boxes, bows and wrapping paper.

One gift is plenty.

Lots of commotion and being passed around and held by visiting friends and relatives may not be in the child's best interest.

Regardless of your religious or holiday traditions, this is not the time to introduce new foods or drinks. This is also a time when we try to dress our kids in cute little outfits for special gatherings, church, etc. Keep in mind that these clothes are not the most comfortable and can tend to make the child irritable. Colds and the flus are abundant at this time as well.

Following are some gift or celebration ideas that can be kept at either home:

- Personalized tree ornaments
- Begin a Christmas Village, adding a new piece each year. This can be displayed and eventually become a tradition to be passed on to the child for his own family in the future.
- Establish a savings account or a lockbox, into which you and others may continually contribute.

Begin a collection of:

- Santa Claus figures
- Elves
- Snowmen
- Angels
- Purchase the Time Life books that detail each year of your child's life.
- Purchase a brick for a new establishment in your child's name.

- Donate to a charitable cause in your child's name, and retain the certificate or receipt as a keepsake.
- Make a memorable scrapbook of the year and your time together, including the receipts and any printed materials associated with places you went and things you did.

Remember:

Give nothing that goes into the mouth or ears.

Do nothing that would take them away from their normal daily activities, i.e., naptime or usual scheduled meals.

Keep your time with them relaxed and loving.

Christmas in their Hometown

The subject of Christmas or Hanukkah is a touchy one with joint custody families.

We should be thankful that the child has the love of both families and that they are wanted in both places to enjoy their traditions.

Expecting the child to straddle between both families is so very stressful. It's like the saying "be in two places at the same time."

If it isn't possible to work things out, here is a fun idea that most kids would enjoy:

Try spending a few days before the holiday with your child in their hometown.

Here are the things you need to pack:

- Thread and a sewing needle
- Scissors (these will have to be checked in your baggage)

- Addresses and phone numbers of friends and relatives
- Tape
- Yarn
- Deck of cards
- Presents
- Hand-held hole punch (for homemade ornaments to be threaded with yarn)

Once you retrieve your child, find the nearest craft store, grocery store, or superstore (your hotel can guide you).

You will purchase the following:

- Small table-top artificial Christmas tree or green poster board to cut into the shape of a Christmas tree to be taped on a wall or door.
- Miniature ornaments for the small table-top tree. Don't forget the hooks or pieces of yarn to hang the ornaments.
- Construction paper, glue and glitter (if you choose to cut out your own ornaments)
- Cardboard holiday cut-outs for the window or door

Food suggestions:

- Microwaveable popcorn
- Fresh cranberries (optional)
- Breakfast food and drinks
- Instant hot cocoa
- Microwaveable slice-and-bake cookies

Back at the hotel, you and your child can set up and decorate a Christmas tree, string popcorn and/or cranberries for the tree, and place other decorations on the door or windows. Designing your own ornaments can be a lot of fun, using glitter, glue and yarn.

Many radio channels or cable TV channels will be playing holiday music.

Together you can make holiday cards to send to your relatives.

You can phone the relatives from your room to wish them all a happy holiday.

Other fun things:

- Order room service or pizza
- Order a holiday movie
- Swim in the hotel pool
- Play games or cards
- Read a story
- Play in the snow

- Put together a holiday jigsaw puzzle

Check with the local parks, recreation department or library to see if there are holiday activities going on in the city, or try something warm indoors such as bowling, playing laser tag or be creative and enjoy a nice ceramic shop. They are creeping up in malls everywhere.

Let the child wake up to your presents under your newly created tree. Kids love the element of surprise.

Give the type of gifts that will require interaction between the two of you and that will give you both something to do the next day, such as:

- Paint-by-numbers sets
- Model car assembly
- Board games
- Tinker Toys or Legos
- Puzzles

Share your childhood memories of the holidays and instill a little family history.

To avoid a sad mood, take the children home prior to un-decorating the tree or let them take the little tree home for their room. Ask them to save it and bring it along next year.

Music, cookies, decorating and presents - what a great holiday!

Other Cool Bonding Ideas

Many internet sites now have the ability to create photo albums uploaded from digital cameras. Providing a camera to older children can help them to send pictures of their life to you or to a website for everyone to enjoy. Photography is a great hobby that can last a lifetime.

This is an awesome past time and provides interaction between all participants in the families. Additionally, it increases their creativity and provides productive time on the internet. Not only does this activity build good computer and communication skills, but has them actively sharing their lives, giving a sensation of good self-worth.

Recordings can now be uploaded and sent directly to phones for up to the minute interaction.

Fabulous technology concepts such as Skype or Yahoo Messenger now make daily interaction so much easier. These are free sources or at the least reasonably inexpensive.

Introducing your child to all the classic books, movies and music is an excellent bonding experience. Whether the two of you are reading or watching together or separately, it still entices the flow of conversation. Encouraging your child to begin journaling is a super tool for their future. Journaling on paper or creating their own blog stimulates their note-taking and writing skills which will benefit their future college and career days. Let them show you the world of Facebook, Twitter and Blogging.

Many family sagas are available in print and movies and provide a lot of education towards a better understanding of life and the world. This increases conversation topics as well as the opportunities to share each other's perspectives. Movies such as Roots, The Immigrants, Little Women, are fun as learning tools but keep up a distant dialogue. It's fun to watch the movies together when you get together again.

Discussions on differences observed between the film version of a story make children begin contrast and comparisons; an excellent intellectual skill. Asking them to describe how they envisioned the character in their minds is an insight for you. You'll be amazed by the differences and similarities you'll share.

The same holds true with historical events of our country, the world and the understanding of the different races of people and the ethnic cultures. Good magazine subscriptions sent to their home or a daily intake of news websites such as CNN or Time Magazine increases their awareness of life as it unfolds and encourages them to share and converse with you, but makes them more insightful in discussions with others and in their education as well.

Make an effort to keep your child informed about your own family history. Although while young it is not usually interesting, they grow to appreciate the information once they are older. They begin to make associations with areas of education, professions and hobbies and it is a sense of connection and grounding for them.

A family memento for your child to cherish or hand-me-downs from family blends the old with the new and gives children a connection to past generations and an understanding of their heritage.

It is suggested to regularly mail cards, letters, postcards or interesting newspaper clippings off to your child. The newspaper clippings or magazine articles that are sent should be of their interest, not just your own. This lets them know you are thinking of them daily and that you do pay attention to their interests. It re-instates your connection together and encourages future discussions.

All of the above mentioned ideas give both a glimpse into each other's passions. The expressing of past experiences and what is known of your heritage is an intimate forecast into both of your future goals and desires. Sharing your dreams and faults with each other is reaching into the depths of the soul. It is why we cherish those long lost relationships of the childhood best friend or that first love. Those people knew us before society took over.

Lastly, never cancel time with them or arrive late. Unless the child has an activity which would warrant an early return, please do not return them home earlier than planned.

Do not divide your time between them and others. Keeping one eye on the game, talking or texting on the phone or computer or taking along a friend of your own age or interest robs the child of their anticipated bonding time. A friend along may inhibit the child from speaking from the heart. It inhibits them from asking any serious questions.

Use your time together for one on one.

In completion of the book, my last words of advice:

Say I love you often!

Tell them how important they are to you.

Hug!

Laugh! Laugh! Laugh!

Epilogue

I hope this book has offered some insight into your child's world and helps to easily Shorten the Distance between you.

My gratitude and best wishes to you and your family. Your comments are encouraged.

Please go to www.ShortenTheDistance.com.

ABOUT THE AUTHOR

A lifetime of visitation!

Dannette Ellenwood Hunnel was an only child of divorced parents by five years of age.

As an adult, Dannette unfortunately found herself also divorced and raising children with long distance parents. Over the years, frustrated by the idea that non-custodial "far away" parents simply call, visit or e-mail, she began writing her emotionally heartfelt thoughts as a form of "therapy." Dannette felt there was so much more in which the other parents could have participated and could have enjoyed together with their children.

Later, Dannette found many people were appreciative of her ideas and experience, encouraging her to put her therapeutic writings into print.

Ms. Hunnel resides with her husband in Phoenix, Arizona, where they enjoy spoiling their growing family.

You can read more at the author's website,

www.ShortenTheDistance.com.

www.ingramcontent.com/pod-product-compliance
Lightning Source LLC
Chambersburg PA
CBHW061653040426
42446CB00010B/1720